Amazing Grace

Illustrated Stories of Favorite Hymns

KENNETH W. OSBECK

Illustrated by David Price

Preface

Every Christian needs an appreciative awareness of God's amazing grace. Through grace God has forgiven us while we were yet sinners and offers us eternal life. Through grace he daily directs us, guides us, and sustains us. Through grace he promises to be with us at life's end to welcome us home.

Yet we forget. We lose the sense of God's presence. We take his amazing grace for granted. How can we remedy this? Spending time in prayer and in studying the Bible are essential. We need to speak to God and hear his trustworthy Word every day.

Another reminder of God's grace that spans the centuries is singing. The church hymnal is a distillation of our collective Christian heritage. Believers have sung out their praises in spiritual songs, in melody, harmony, and rhythm down through the ages. Through hymns we can find expression for our own feelings of awe, worship, and gratitude. Through their memorable verses we can be inspired to remember, every minute of our lives, our good God and his amazing grace.

Contents

AMAZING GRACE

John Newton, 1725–1807 (verses 1–4), John P. Rees, 1828–1900 (verse 5)

And God is able to make all grace abound to you, so that in all things at all times . . .
you will abound in every good work. (2 Corinthians 9:8)

Amazing Grace tune   American melody from *Carrell & Clayton's Virginia Harmony*, 1831

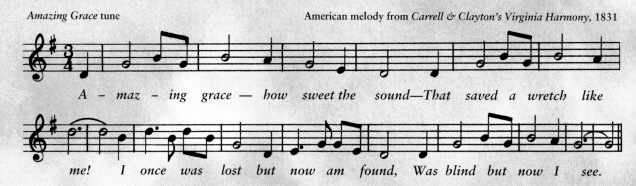

A – maz – ing grace — how sweet the sound—That saved a wretch like me! I once was lost but now am found, Was blind but now I see.

Amazing grace—how sweet the sound—
That saved a wretch like me!
I once was lost but now am found,
Was blind but now I see.

'Twas grace that taught my heart to fear,
And grace my fears relieved;
How precious did that grace appear
The hour I first believed!

Thru many dangers, toils and snares
I have already come;
'Tis grace hath brought me safe thus far,
And grace will lead me home.

The Lord has promised good to me;
His word my hope secures;
He will my shield and portion be
As long as life endures.

When we've been there ten thousand years,
Bright shining as the sun,
We've no less days to sing God's praise
Than when we'd first begun.

Calling himself a "wretch" who was lost and blind, John Newton recalled leaving school at the age of eleven to begin life as a rough, debauched seaman. Eventually he engaged in the despicable practice of capturing natives from West Africa to be sold as slaves to markets around the world. But one day the grace of God put fear into the heart of this wicked slave trader through a fierce storm. Greatly alarmed and fearful of a shipwreck, Newton began to read *The Imitation of Christ* by Thomas à Kempis. God used this book to lead him to a genuine conversion and a dramatic change in his way of life.

Feeling a definite call to study for the ministry, Newton was encouraged and greatly influenced by John and Charles Wesley and George Whitefield. At the age of thirty-nine, John Newton became an ordained minister of the Anglican church at the little village of Olney, near Cambridge, England. To add further impact to his powerful preaching, Newton introduced simple heart-felt hymns rather than the usual psalms in his services. When enough hymns could not be found, Newton began to write his own, often assisted by his close friend William Cowper. In 1779 their combined efforts produced the famous *Olney Hymns* hymnal. "Amazing Grace" was from that collection.

Until the time of his death at the age of eighty-two, John Newton never ceased to marvel at the grace of God that transformed him so completely. Shortly before his death he is quoted as proclaiming with a loud voice during a message, "My memory is nearly gone, but I remember two things: That I am a great sinner and that Christ is a great Savior!" What amazing grace!

For Today

1 Chronicles 17:16–17; John 1:16–17; Romans 5:20–21

Ponder anew the magnitude of God's grace.

John Newton.

7

A MIGHTY FORTRESS

Words and Music by Martin Luther, 1483–1546
English Translation by Frederick H. Hedge, 1805–1890

God is our refuge and strength, an ever present help in trouble. Therefore we will not fear, though the earth give way and the mountains fall into the heart of the sea. (Psalm 46:1–2)

Ein Fest' Burg tune

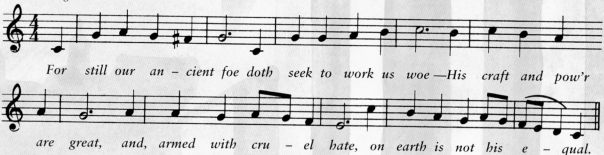

For still our an – cient foe doth seek to work us woe —His craft and pow'r

are great, and, armed with cru – el hate, on earth is not his e – qual.

A mighty fortress is our God,
a bulwark never failing;
our helper He amid the flood
of mortal ills prevailing.
For still our ancient foe
doth seek to work us woe—
His craft and pow'r are great,
and, armed with cruel hate,
on earth is not his equal.

Did we in our own strength confide
our striving would be losing,
were not the right Man on our side,
the Man of God's own choosing.
Dost ask who that may be?
Christ Jesus, it is He—
Lord Sabaoth His name,
from age to age the same—
and He must win the battle.

October 31, 1517, is perhaps the most important day in Protestant history. This was the day when Martin Luther, an Augustinian monk and a professor of theology, posted on the doors of the Cathedral of Wittenberg, Germany, his Ninety-Five theses (complaints) against the teachings and practices of the medieval Roman Church. With this event, the sixteenth-century Protestant Reformation was formally born.

The Protestant Reformation movement was built on three main tenets:

• The re-establishment of the Scriptures.
• Clarifying the means of salvation.
• The restoration of congregational singing.

"A Mighty Fortress" was written and composed by Martin Luther. The date of the hymn cannot be fixed with any exact

8

certainty. It is generally believed, however, to have been written for the Diet of Spires in 1529 when the term "protestant" was first used. The hymn became the great rallying cry of the Reformation.

For Today

Deuteronomy 33:27; 2 Samuel 22:2; Psalm 46; Isaiah 26:4

Breathe a prayer of thanks to God for Reformers such as Martin Luther, who laid the foundations for our evangelical faith.

Martin Luther.

COUNT YOUR BLESSINGS

Johnson Oatman, Jr., 1856–1922

Praise be to the God and Father of our Lord Jesus Christ, who has blessed us in the heavenly realms with every spiritual blessing in Christ. (Ephesians 1:3)

Edwin O. Excell, 1851–1921

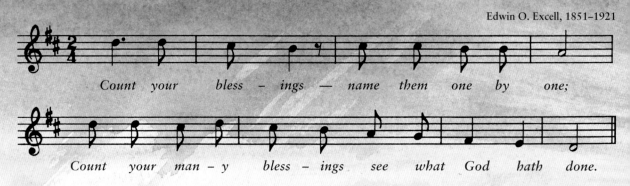

Count your bless - ings — name them one by one;

Count your man - y bless - ings see what God hath done.

When upon life's billows you are tempest tossed,
when you are discouraged, thinking all is lost,
count your many blessings—name them
      one by one,
and it will surprise you what the Lord hath done.

Are you ever burdened with a load of care?
Does the cross seem heavy you are called to bear?
Count your many blessings—ev'ry doubt will fly,
and you will be singing as the days go by.

When you look at others with their lands and gold,
think that Christ has promised you His
      wealth untold;
count your many blessings—money cannot buy
your reward in heaven nor your home on high.

So amid the conflict, whether great or small,
do not be discouraged. God is over all;
count your many blessings—angels will attend,
help and comfort give you to your journey's end.

CHORUS:
Count your blessings—name them one by one;
count your blessings—see what God hath done.

For the Christian, gratitude should be a life attitude. "Count Your Blessings" was written by one of the prolific gospel song writers of the past century, a Methodist lay preacher named Johnson Oatman. In addition to his preaching and the writing of more than five thousand hymn texts, Oatman was also a successful businessman engaged in a shipping business, and in his later years an administrator for a large insurance company in New Jersey.

It is good for each of us periodically to take time to rediscover the simple but profound truths expressed by Mr. Oatman in the four stanzas of this hymn. In the first two verses he develops the thought that counting our blessings serves as an antidote for life's discouragements and in turn makes for victorious Christian living. The third stanza of this hymn teaches us that counting our blessings can be a means of placing material possessions in proper perspective when

compared to the eternal inheritance awaiting believers. Then, as we review our individual blessings, we certainly would have to agree with Mr. Oatman's fourth verse: The provision of God's help and comfort at the end of our earthly pilgrimage is one of our choicest blessings.

Each of us could spare ourselves much despair and inner tension if we would only learn to apply the practical teaching of this hymn to our daily living.

Johnson Oatman Jr.

For Today

Psalm 28:7, 68:19, 69:30–31; James 1:17

Make a list of God's blessings. Share this list with your friends and family.

11

BLESSED ASSURANCE

Fanny J. Crosby, 1820–1915

Let us draw near to God with a sincere heart in full assurance of faith, having our hearts sprinkled to cleanse us from a guilty conscience and having our bodies washed with pure water. Let us hold unswervingly to the hope we profess, for He who promised is faithful. (Hebrews 10:22–23)

Beware of despairing about yourself. You are commanded to put your trust in God, and not in yourself. —St. Augustine

Phoebe P. Knapp, 1839–1908

This is my sto-ry, this is my song, Prais-ing my Sav-ior all the day long.

Blessed assurance, Jesus is mine!
O what a foretaste of glory divine!
Heir of salvation, purchase of God,
born of His Spirit, washed in His blood.

Perfect submission, perfect delight!
Visions of rapture now burst on my sight;
angels descending bring from above
echoes of mercy, whispers of love.

Perfect submission—all is at rest;
I in my Savior am happy and blest;
watching and waiting, looking above,
filled with His goodness, lost in His love.

CHORUS:
This is my story, this is my song,
praising my Savior all the day long;
this is my story, this is my song,
praising my Savior all the day long.

Some people claim to have accepted Christ as Savior, yet they live in the tragic uncertainty of doubting their personal relationship with God. The Scriptures teach, however, that we can know with absolute confidence that we have the life of God within us (1 John 5:13). This confidence is not based on inner feelings or outer signs. Rather, this assurance is founded upon the promises of a faithful God and His inspired Word. It depends not on the amount of our faith but on the object of our faith—Christ Himself.

Though blinded at six weeks of age through improper medical treatment, Fanny Crosby wrote more than eight thousand gospel songs texts in her lifetime of ninety-five years. Her many favorites such as "Blessed Assurance" have been an important part of evangelical worship for the past century. Only eternity will disclose the host of individuals whose lives have been spiritually enriched through the texts of Fanny Crosby's many hymns. Engraved on Fanny J. Crosby's tombstone at Bridgeport, Connecticut, are these significant words taken from our Lord's remarks to Mary, the sister of Lazarus, after she had anointed Him with costly perfume—"She hath done what she could" (Mark 14:8).

For Today

Isaiah 12:2; Romans 8:16–17, 15:13; Titus 2:13–14; 1 John 5:13; Revelation 1:5–6

If you have accepted Christ as personal Savior, live with the absolute conviction and triumphant faith that the apostle Paul had when he exclaimed, "I know whom [not merely what] I have believed" (2 Timothy 1:12).

Fanny J. Crosby.

13

GREAT IS THY FAITHFULNESS

Thomas O. Chisholm, 1866–1960

Because of the Lord's great love we are not consumed, for His compassions never fail. They are new every morning; great is Your Faithfulness. (Lamentations 3:22–23)

William M. Runyan, 1870–1957

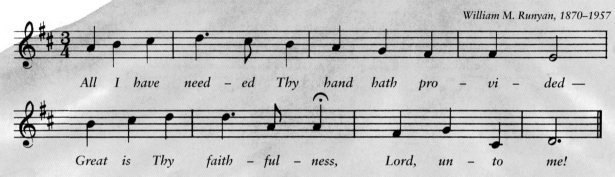

All I have need - ed Thy hand hath pro - vi - ded —

Great is Thy faith - ful - ness, Lord, un - to me!

Great is Thy faithfulness, O God my Father!
There is no shadow of turning with Thee;
Thou changest not; Thy compassions, they fail not:
As thou hast been Thou forever wilt be.

Summer and winter, and springtime and harvest,
sun, moon and stars in their courses above,
join with all nature in manifold witness
to Thy great faithfulness, mercy and love.

Pardon for sin and a peace that endureth,
thine own dear presence to cheer and to guide,
strength for today and bright hope for tomorrow—
blessings all mine, with ten thousand beside.

CHORUS:
Great is Thy faithfulness! Great is Thy
*   faithfulness!*
Morning by morning new mercies I see;
all I have needed Thy hand hath provided—
Great is Thy faithfulness, Lord, unto me.

One of the important lessons the Children of Israel had to learn during their wilderness journey was that God's provision of manna for them was on a morning by morning basis. They could not survive on old manna nor could it be stored for future use (Exodus 16:19–21).

While many enduring hymns are born out of a particular dramatic experience, this was simply the result of the author's "morning by morning" realization of God's personal faithfulness in his daily life. Shortly before his death in 1960, Thomas Chisholm wrote:

My income has never been large at any time due to impaired health in the earlier years which has followed me on until now. But I must not fail to record here the unfailing faithfulness of a covenant keeping God and that He has given me many wonderful displays of His providing care which have filled me with astonishing gratefulness.

Thomas Obadiah Chisholm was born in a crude log cabin in Franklin, Kentucky. From this humble beginning and without the benefit of high school or advanced education, he somehow began his career as a school teacher at the age of sixteen in the same country school where he had received his elementary training. After accepting Christ as Savior, he became editor of *The Pentecostal Herald* and later was ordained as a Methodist minister. Throughout his long lifetime, Mr. Chisholm wrote more than 1,200 sacred poems, many of which have since become prominent hymn texts.

Thomas O. Chisholm.

For Today

Psalm 9:10; 36:5–7; 102:11–12; James 1:17

Live with this spirit of grateful praise.

HAVE THINE OWN WAY, LORD

Adelaide A. Pollard, 1862–1934

Yet, O Lord, you are our Father. We are the clay, You are the potter; we are all the work of Your hand. (Isaiah 64:8)

Adelaide tune   George C. Stebbins, 1846–1945

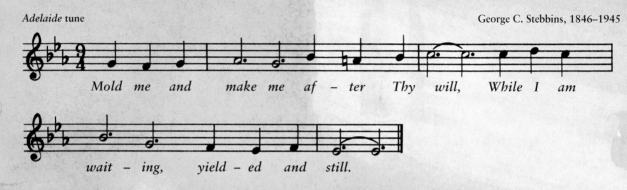

Mold me and make me af — ter Thy will, While I am wait — ing, yield — ed and still.

Have Thine own way, Lord! Have Thine own way!
Thou art the potter, I am the clay.
Mold me and make me after Thy will,
while I am waiting, yielded and still.

Have Thine own way, Lord! Have Thine own way!
Search me and try me, Master, today!
Whiter than snow, Lord, wash me just now,
as in Thy presence humbly I bow.

Have Thine own way, Lord! Have Thine own way!
Wounded and weary, help me, I pray!
Power, all power, surely is Thine!
Touch me and heal me, Savior divine!

Have Thine own way, Lord! Have Thine own way!
Hold o'er my being absolute sway!
Fill with Thy Spirit till all shall see
Christ only, always, living in me!

An elderly woman at a prayer meeting one night pleaded, "It really doesn't matter what you do with us, Lord, just have your way with our lives." At this meeting was Adelaide Pollard, a rather well-known itinerant Bible teacher who was deeply discouraged because she had been unable to raise the necessary funds for a desired trip to Africa to do missionary service. She was moved by the older woman's sincere and dedicated request of God.

At home that evening Miss Pollard meditated on Jeremiah 18:3–4:

Then I went down to the potter's house, and behold, he wrought a work on the wheels, and the vessel that he made of clay was marred in the hand of the potter; so he made it again another vessel, as seemed good to the potter to make it.

16

Before retiring that evening, Adelaide Pollard completed the writing of all four stanzas of this hymn as it is sung today. The hymn first appeared in published form in 1907.

Often into our lives come discouragements and heartaches that we cannot understand. As children of God, however, we must learn never to question the ways of our sovereign God— but simply to say, "Have Thine own way, Lord."

For Today

Psalm 27:14; Romans 6:13–14, 9:20–21; Galatians 2:20

Reflect on this ancient prayer: "I am willing, Lord, to receive what Thou givest, to lack what Thou withholdest, to relinquish what Thou takest, to surrender what Thou claimest, to suffer what Thou ordainest, to do what Thou commandest, to wait until Thou sayest 'Go.'"

SOLDIERS OF CHRIST, ARISE

Charles Wesley, 1707–1788

Finally, be strong in the Lord and in His mighty power. Put on the full armor of God so that you can take your stand against the devil's schemes. (Ephesians 6:10–11).

Diademata tune   George J. Elvey, 1816–1893

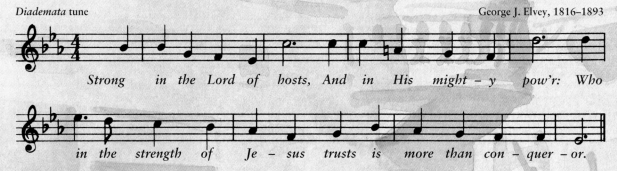

Strong in the Lord of hosts, And in His might – y pow'r: Who

in the strength of Je – sus trusts is more than con – quer – or.

*Soldiers of Christ, arise
and put your armor on,
strong in the strength which God supplies
thru His eternal Son;
strong in the Lord of hosts
and in His mighty pow'r:
Who in the strength of Jesus trusts
is more than conqueror.*

*Stand then in His great might,
with all His strength endued,
and take, to arm you for the fight,
the panoply of God;
that having all things done,
and all your conflicts past,
ye may o'ercome thru Christ alone
and stand entire at last.*

*Leave no unguarded place,
no weakness of the soul;
take ev'ry virtue, ev'ry grace,
and fortify the whole.
From strength to strength go on;
Wrestle and fight and pray;
tread all the pow'rs of darkness down
and win the well-fought day.*

Followers of Christ are also His soldiers—called to do battle with the forces of Satan and evil. Victories are never won while resting in the barracks. God's soldiers must always be alert and dressed in full armor. That armor includes six important pieces (Ephesians 6:10–20):

1. The belt of truth (warriors with absolute integrity).
2. The breastplate of righteousness (people must see our good works).
3. Sandals of peace (though soldiers, we are called to be peacemakers).
4. Shield of faith (for extinguishing all of Satan's doubts and fears).
5. Helmet of salvation (one of Satan's chief attacks is the mind).
6. Sword of the Spirit—the Word of God (our only offensive weapon).

In addition to wearing armor, the Christian soldier is to face every occasion with prayer and to remember the fellow saints in prayer (v. 18). Ultimately, however, the battle is not ours but God's (2 Chronicles 20:15). He knows the battle plan. Our responsibility is only to be active and obedient in the small duty wherever He has placed us on the battlefield.

Charles Wesley knew much about the Christian life as warfare. Many times both John and Charles were physically abused for their evangelical ministries. This text was first published in 1749 and was titled "The Whole Armor of God—Ephesians VI." The hymn has often been referred to as "the Christian's bugle blast" for its strong call to arms.

For Today

1 Corinthians 15:57–58; Ephesians 6:10–20; Philippians 1:27–30; 1 Timothy 6:12

Reflect on the words of Maltbie D. Babcock—"We are not here to play, to dream, to drift; we have hard work to do, and loads to lift. Shun not the struggle; face it—'tis God's gift." Go forth in your full armor and in the power of His might.

Charles Wesley.

THE OLD RUGGED CROSS

Words and Music by George Bennard, 1873–1958

He Himself bore our sins in His body on the tree, so that we might die to sins and live for righteousness; by His wounds you have been healed. (1 Peter 2:24)

So I'll cher–ish the old rug–ged cross, Till my tro–phies at last I lay down;

I will cling to the old rug–ged cross, And ex–change it some day for a crown.

On a hill far away stood an old rugged cross,
the emblem of suff'ring and shame;
and I love that old cross where the dearest and best
for a world of lost sinners was slain.

O that old rugged cross, so despised by the world,
has a wondrous attraction for me;
for the dear Lamb of God left His glory above
to bear it to dark Calvary.

To the old rugged cross I will ever be true,
its shame and reproach gladly bear;
then He'll call me some day to my home far away,
where His glory forever I'll share.

CHORUS:
So I'll cherish the old rugged cross,
till my trophies at last I lay down;
I will cling to the old rugged cross,
and exchange it some day for a crown.

The author and composer of this beloved hymn, George Bennard, began his Christian ministry in the ranks of the Salvation Army. Eight years later he was ordained by the Methodist Episcopal church, where his devoted ministry as an evangelist was highly esteemed for many years.

One time, after returning to his home in Albion, Michigan, Bennard passed through a particularly trying experience, one that caused him to reflect seriously about the significance of the cross and what the apostle Paul meant when he spoke of entering into the fellowship of Christ's sufferings (Philippians 3:10). George Bennard began to spend long hours in study, prayer, and meditation until one day he could say:

I saw the Christ of the cross as if I were seeing John 3:16 leave the printed page, take form and act out the meaning of redemption. The more I contemplated these truths the more convinced I became that the cross was far more than just a religious symbol but rather the very heart of the gospel.

During these days of spiritual struggle, the theme for "The Old Rugged Cross" began to formulate itself in Bennard's mind. But an inner voice seemed to keep telling him to wait. Finally, however, after returning to Michigan, he began to concentrate anew on his project. This time the words and melody began to flow easily from his heart. Shortly thereafter, Bennard sent a manuscript copy to Charles Gabriel, one of the leading gospel hymn writers of that time. Gabriel's prophetic words, "You will certainly hear from this song, Mr. Bennard," were soon realized as the hymn became one of the most widely published songs, either sacred or secular, throughout America.

George Bennard.

For Today

Isaiah 53:3–12; John 19:17–25; Romans 5:6–11; Hebrews 9:27–28

Ponder the significance of Christ's cross in your salvation.

21

HIS NAME IS WONDERFUL

Words and Music by Audrey Mieir, b. 1916

For unto us a child is born, unto us a son is given, and the government shall be upon His shoulder; and His name shall be called Wonderful, Counselor, the Mighty God, the Everlasting Father, The Prince of Peace. (Isaiah 9:6 KJV)

He is the might–y King, Mas–ter of ev–'ry–thing;

His name is Won–der–ful, Je–sus, my Lord.

His name is Wonderful, His name is Wonderful,
His name is Wonderful, Jesus, my Lord;
He is the mighty King,
Master of ev'rything;
His name is Wonderful, Jesus, my Lord.

He's the great Shepherd, the Rock of all ages,
Almighty God is He;
bow down before Him,
love and adore Him;
His name is Wonderful, Jesus my Lord.

More than 2,500 years ago, the prophet Isaiah told of One who would be the hope of mankind, the long-awaited Messiah who would establish an eternal kingdom based on justice and righteousness. Isaiah's important pronouncement told that this one would be a God-man: a child born— His humanity; a son given—His deity. The quintuplet of names ascribed to this One gives further insight into His character and ministry:

- Wonderful—He would be wonderful in what He would accomplish for the fallen human race.
- Counselor—He would be our guide through life and our advocate before the heavenly Father.
- The Mighty God—He would be the God before whom every knee shall one day bow.
- The Everlasting Father—He would be the God of eternity.
- The Prince of Peace—He would be the one who would ultimately bring a true tranquility among all nations.

Audrey Mieir has been widely known for several decades as the composer and author of many fine gospel songs and choruses. "His Name Is Wonderful," written in 1959, is one of her finest. She tells in her biography how the inspiration for this song occurred while she watched the annual Christmas program given at her Bethel Union Church in Duarte, California. After the usual procession of angels, shepherds, Mary and Joseph, the singing of "sleep in heavenly peace," the pastor of the church suddenly exclaimed—"His name is wonderful." Audrey Mieir tells that she quickly grabbed her Bible, searched the concordance for names given to Jesus in the Scriptures, and soon composed this song, which has since been sung around the world.

Audrey Mieir.

For Today

Psalm 72:19; Proverbs 18:10, 22:1; John 1:12; Acts 4:12; Philippians 2:9–10

The more intimately we know the "child-Son," the deeper grows our love and devotion for Him.

23

HOLY, HOLY, HOLY

Reginald Heber, 1783–1826

Come, let us bow down in worship, let us kneel before the Lord our Maker; for He is our God and we are the people of His pasture, the flock under His care. (Psalm 95:6–7)

"O Lord, grant that I may desire Thee, and desiring Thee, seek Thee, and seeking Thee, find Thee, and finding Thee, be satisfied with Thee forever."
—St. Augustine

Nicaea tune
John B. Dykes, 1823–1876

Ho - ly, Ho - ly, Ho - ly! Mer - ci - ful and Migh - ty! God in Three Per - sons, bless - ed Trin - i - ty.

Holy, Holy, Holy, Lord God Almighty!
Early in the morning our song shall rise to Thee;
Holy, Holy, Holy! Merciful and Mighty!
God in Three Persons, blessed Trinity!

Holy, Holy, Holy! All the saints adore Thee,
casting down their golden crowns around the
*   glassy sea;*
cherubim and seraphim falling down before Thee,
which wert and art and evermore shalt be.

Holy, Holy, Holy! Tho the darkness hide Thee,
tho the eye of sinful man Thy glory may not see.
Only Thou art holy—there is none beside Thee
perfect in pow'r, in love and purity.

Holy, Holy, Holy, Lord God Almighty!
All Thy works shall praise Thy name in earth and
*   sky and sea;*
Holy, Holy, Holy! Merciful and Mighty!
God in Three Persons, blessed Trinity!

"Holy, holy, holy is the Lord God Almighty who was, and is, and is to come" (Revelation 4:8). These are the words of worship that believers will proclaim in heaven one day. This majestic hymn text based on these words was written approximately one hundred and fifty years ago by an Anglican minister, Reginald Heber, and it is still one of the hymns most frequently used in our corporate worship.

Worship is the cornerstone of a believer's spiritual life. The bedrock of the local church is its worship service, and all aspects of the church's ministry are founded here. It is only as a Christian truly worships that he begins to grow spiritually. Learning to worship and praise God, then, should be a believer's lifetime pursuit. Our worship reflects the depth of our relationship with God. We must learn to worship God not only for what He is doing in our personal lives, but above all, for who He is—His being, character, and deeds.

Reginald Heber was a highly respected minister, writer, and church leader, serving for a time as the Bishop of Calcutta. His early death at the age of forty-three was widely mourned throughout the Christian world. One year after his death, a collection of fifty-seven of his hymns was published by his widow and many friends as a tribute to his memory and faithful ministry. It is from this collection of 1827 that this hymn was taken.

Reginald Heber.

For Today

Psalm 145:8–21; Isaiah 6:3; Revelation 4:5–11, 5:13

What does the term "worship" mean to you? How could your life of worship be improved? Use this hymn to help you achieve more intimate, meaningful worship with our holy God.

IT IS WELL WITH MY SOUL

Horatio E. Spafford, 1828–1888

God is our refuge and strength, an ever present help in trouble. (Psalm 46:1)

Philip P. Bliss, 1838–1876

It is well.... with my soul,..... It is well, it is well with my soul.

When peace, like a river, attendeth my way,
when sorrows like sea billows roll—
Whatever my lot, Thou hast taught me to say,
It is well, it is well with my soul.

Tho Satan should buffet, tho trials should come,
let this blest assurance control,
that Christ hath regarded my helpless estate
and shed His own blood for my soul.

And, Lord, haste the day when my faith
     shall be sight,
the clouds be rolled back as a scroll:
The trump shall resound and the Lord
     shall descend,
"Even so"—it is well with my soul.

CHORUS:
It is well with my soul,
it is well, it is well with my soul.

Inner peace through an implicit trust in the love of God is the real evidence of a mature Christian faith. Only with this kind of confidence in his heavenly Father could Horatio Spafford experience such heart-rending tragedies as he did and yet be able to say, "It is well with my soul."

Spafford had known peaceful and happy days as a successful attorney in Chicago. He was the father of four daughters, an active member of the Presbyterian church, and a loyal friend and supporter of D. L. Moody and other evangelical leaders of his day. Then, a series of calamities began, starting with the great Chicago fire of 1871 that wiped out the family's extensive real estate investments. When Mr. Moody and his music associate, Ira Sankey, left for Great Britain for an evangelistic campaign, Spafford decided to lift the spirits of his family by taking them on a vacation to Europe. He also planned to assist in the Moody-Sankey meetings there.

In November 1873, Spafford was detained by urgent business, but he sent his wife and four daughters as scheduled on the S.S. *Ville du Harve*, planning to join them soon.

26

Halfway across the Atlantic, the ship was struck by an English vessel and sank in twelve minutes. All four of the Spafford daughters—Tanetta, Maggie, Annie, and Bessie—were among the 226 who drowned. Mrs. Spafford was among the few who were miraculously saved.

Horatio Spafford stood hour after hour on the deck of the ship carrying him to rejoin his sorrowing wife in Cardiff, Wales. When the ship passed the approximate place where his precious daughters had drowned, Spafford received sustaining comfort from God that enabled him to write, "When sorrows like sea billows roll . . . It is well with my soul." What a picture of hope!

Horatio E. Spafford.

For Today

Psalm 31:14, 142:3; Galatians 2:20; 1 Peter 4:19

Ask yourself if you can truthfully say, "It is well with my soul," no matter what the circumstances may be that surround you.

JUST AS I AM

Charlotte Elliott, 1789–1871

Then Jesus declared, "I am the bread of life. He who comes to Me will never go hungry, and he who believes in Me will never be thirsty. All that the Father gives Me will come to Me, and whoever comes to Me I will never drive away." (John 6:35, 37)

Woodworth tune   William B. Bradbury, 1816–1868

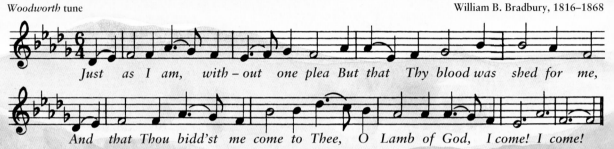

Just as I am, with-out one plea But that Thy blood was shed for me,
And that Thou bidd'st me come to Thee, O Lamb of God, I come! I come!

*Just as I am, without one plea
but that Thy blood was shed for me,
and that Thou bidd'st me come to Thee,
O Lamb of God, I come! I come!*

*Just as I am, tho tossed about
with many a conflict, many a doubt,
fightings and fears within, without,
O Lamb of God, I come! I come!*

*Just as I am, poor, wretched, blind—
Sight, riches, healing of the mind,
yea, all I need in Thee to find—
O Lamb of God, I come! I come!*

*Just as I am, Thou wilt receive,
wilt welcome, pardon, cleanse, relieve;
because Thy promise I believe,
O Lamb of God, I come! I come!*

Often we feel that if only we were in different circumstances or had some special talent, we could be a better witness for God and serve Him more effectively. Today's hymn was written by a bed-ridden invalid who felt useless to do anything except express her feelings of devotion to God. Yet Charlotte Elliott's simply worded text has influenced more people for Christ than any hymn ever written or perhaps any sermon ever preached.

As a young person in Brighton, England, Miss Elliott was known as "carefree Charlotte." She was a popular portrait artist and a writer of humorous verse. At the age of thirty, however, a serious ailment made her an invalid for life. She became listless and depressed until a well-known Swiss evangelist, Dr. Caesar Malan, visited her. Sensing her spiritual distress, he exclaimed, "Charlotte, you must come just as you are—a sinner—to the Lamb of God who takes away the sin of the world!" Immediately placing her complete trust in Christ's redemptive sacrifice for her, Charlotte experienced inner peace and joy in spite of her physical affliction, until her death at the age of eighty-two.

Charlotte Elliott wrote approximately one hundred and fifty hymns throughout her lifetime; today she is considered to be one of the finest of all English hymnwriters. "God sees, God guards, God guides me," she said. "His grace surrounds me and His voice continually bids me to be happy and holy in His service—just where I am!"

Charlotte Elliott.

For Today

Psalm 51:1–2; John 1:29, 3:16; Ephesians 2:13

Give God thanks for His acceptance of us just as we are. As we respond in simple faith to Him, we will find "all that we need," not only for our personal salvation but also for the particular place of service that He has for us.

29

NOW THANK WE ALL OUR GOD

Martin Rinkart, 1586–1649
English Translation by Catherine Winkworth, 1827–1878

Who shall separate us from the love of Christ? Shall trouble or hardship or persecution or famine or nakedness or danger or sword? No, in all these things we are more than conquerors through Him who loved us. (Romans 8:35, 37)

Nun Danket tune   Johann Crüger, 1598–1662

Now thank we all our God with hearts and hands and voic–es; Who from our moth–ers' arms hath blessed us on our way—And still is ours to - day.

Now thank we all our God
with hearts and hands and voices,
who wondrous things hath done,
in whom His world rejoices;
who from our mothers' arms
hath blessed us on our way
with countless gifts of love,
and still is ours today.

O may this bounteous God
thru all our life be near us,
with ever joyful hearts
and blessed peace to cheer us;
and keep us in His grace,
and guide us when perplexed,
and free us from all ills
in this world and the next.

From some of the severest human sufferings imaginable during the Thirty Years' War of 1618–48, a war that has been described as the most devastating in all history, this great hymn of the church was born.

Martin Rinkart was called at the age of thirty-one to pastor the state Lutheran church in his native city of Eilenberg, Germany. He arrived there just as the dreadful bloodshed of the Thirty Years' War began, and there Rinkart spent the remaining thirty-two years of his life faithfully ministering to these needy people.

Germany, the battleground of this conflict between warring Catholic and Protestant forces from various countries throughout Europe, was reduced to a state of misery beyond description. The German population dwindled from 16 million to 6 million. Because Eilenberg

30

was a walled city, it became a frightfully over-crowded refuge for political and military fugitives from far and near. Throughout these war years several waves of deadly diseases and famines swept the city as the various armies marched through the town, leaving death and destruction in their wake. The plague of 1637 was particularly severe. At its height Rinkart was the only minister remaining to care for the sick and dying.

Martin Rinkart's triumphant, personal expressions of gratitude and confidence in God confirm for each of us this truth taught in Scripture, that as God's children, we too can be "more than conquerors through Him who loved us."

For Today

1 Chronicles 16:36; Psalm 147; 1 Corinthians 15:57–58

God wants us to be victors and not the victims of life. With His presence we can overcome and not be overwhelmed.

Martin Rinkart

31

O COME, O COME, EMMANUEL

Latin hymn from 12th century
English Translation by John M. Neale, 1818–1866

He will be great and will be called the Son of the Most High. The Lord God will give Him the throne of His father David, and He will reign over the house of Jacob forever; His kingdom will never end. (Luke 1:32–33)

Veni Emmanuel tune

Plainsong, 13th century

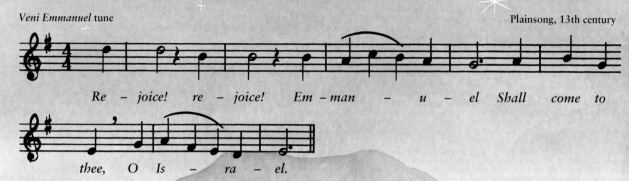

Re – joice! re – joice! Em – man – u – el Shall come to

thee, O Is – ra – el.

O come, O come, Emmanuel,
and ransom captive Israel,
that mourns in lonely exile here
until the Son of God appear.

O come, O come, Thou Lord of might
who to Thy tribes, on Sinai's height,
in ancient times didst give the law
in cloud and majesty and awe.

O come, Thou Day-spring, come and cheer
our spirits by Thine advent here;
O drive away the shades of night
and pierce the clouds and bring us light.

O come, Thou Key of David, come
and open wide our heav'nly home
where all Thy saints with Thee shall dwell—
O come, O come, Emmanuel!

REFRAIN:
Rejoice! rejoice!
Emmanuel shall come to thee, O Israel.

The preparation for the celebration of our Lord's birth begins four Sundays before Christmas Day. This begins the period known as the Advent season. Advent centers on the Old Testament prophecies concerning a coming Messiah and His establishment of an earthly kingdom.

The Messiah's coming was prophesied six hundred years before His birth. At the time the Jewish people were living in captivity in Babylon. For centuries thereafter faithful Jews earnestly anticipated the Deliverer-Messiah with great longing and expectation, echoing the prayer that He would "ransom captive Israel." And finally the long-awaited heavenly announcement came—"Unto you is born this day in the city of David a Savior, which is Christ the Lord!" (Luke 2:11).

"O Come, O Come, Emmanuel" was

originally used in the medieval church liturgy as a series of antiphons—short musical statements that were sung for the week of vesper services just before Christmas Eve. Each of these antiphons greets the anticipated Messiah with one of the titles ascribed Him throughout the Old Testament: Wisdom, Emmanuel, the Lord of Might, the Rod of Jesse, Day Spring, and the Key of David.

The haunting modal melody for the verses is also of ancient origin. It is based on one of the earliest forms of sacred music known—the chant or plain song.

John M. Neale.

For Today

Isaiah 7:14, 9:6, 11:1, 22:22; Matthew 1:22–23; Luke 1:78–79; Galatians 4:45

Christ came not only to be the Emmanuel—"God with us"—but also to be God in us. Carry this truth throughout the Advent season and the year.

33

ABIDE WITH ME

Henry F. Lyte, 1793–1847

But they constrained Him, saying, "Abide with us: for it is toward evening, and the day is far spent."
And He went in to tarry with them. (Luke 24:29 KJV)

Yes, life is like the Emmaus road, and we tread it not alone
For beside us walks the Son of God, to uphold and keep His own.
And our hearts within us thrill with joy at His words of love and grace,
And the glorious hope that when day is done we shall see His blessed face.

—Avis Christiansen

Eventide tune

William H. Monk, 1823–1889

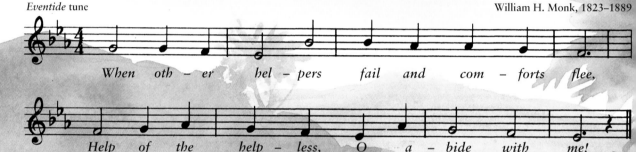

When oth – er hel – pers fail and com – forts flee,

Help of the help – less, O a – bide with me!

Abide with me—fast falls the eventide.
The darkness deepens—Lord, with me abide;
when other helpers fail and comforts flee,
help of the helpless, O abide with me!

Swift to its close ebbs out life's little day;
earth's joys grow dim; its glories pass away;
change and decay in all around I see—
O Thou who changest not, abide with me!

I need Thy presence ev'ry passing hour—
What but Thy grace can foil the tempter's pow'r?
Who like Thyself my guide and stay can be?
Thru cloud and sunshine, O abide with me.

Hold Thou Thy word before my closing eyes.
Shine thru the gloom and point me to the skies;
heav'n's morning breaks and earth's vain
           shadows flee—
In life, in death, O Lord, abide with me.

The author of this text, Henry F. Lyte, was an Anglican pastor. Though he battled tuberculosis all of his life, Lyte was known as a man strong in spirit and faith. It was he who coined the phrase "it is better to wear out than to rust out."

During his later years, Lyte's health progressively worsened so that he was forced to seek a warmer climate in Italy. For the last sermon with his parishioners at Lower Brixham, England, on September 4, 1847, it is recorded that he nearly had to crawl to the pulpit. His final words made a deep impact upon his people when he proclaimed, "It is my desire to induce you to prepare for the solemn hour which must come to all, by a timely appreciation and dependence on the death of Christ."

Henry Lyte's inspiration for writing "Abide with Me" came shortly before his final sermon, while reading from the account in Luke 24 of our Lord's appearance with the two disciples on their seven-mile walk from Jerusalem to the village of Emmaus on that first Easter evening. How the hearts of those discouraged disciples suddenly burned within them when they realized that they were in the company of the risen, eternal Son of God!

For Today

Psalm 139:7–12; Luke 24:13–35; 1 John 3:24

Relive the thrill expressed by the two Emmaus disciples when their spiritual eyes were opened and they first realized that they were in the presence of their risen Lord.

Henry F. Lyte.

35

O GOD, OUR HELP IN AGES PAST

Isaac Watts, 1674–1748

Lord, You have been our dwelling place throughout all generations. Before the mountains were born or You brought forth the earth and the world, from everlasting to everlasting You are God. (Psalm 90:1–2)

St. Anne tune   Attributed to William Croft, 1678–1727

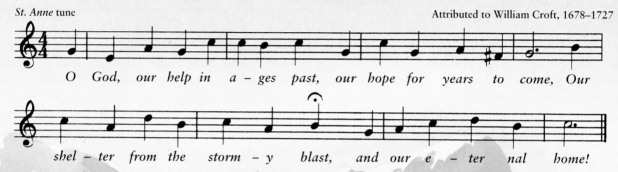

O God, our help in a – ges past, our hope for years to come, Our
shel – ter from the storm – y blast, and our e – ter nal home!

O God, our help in ages past,
our hope for years to come,
our shelter from the stormy blast,
and our eternal home.

Under the shadow of Thy throne
still may we dwell secure;
sufficient is Thine arm alone,
and our defense is sure.

Before the hills in order stood
or earth received her frame,
from everlasting Thou art God,
to endless years the same.

Time, like an ever rolling stream,
bears all its sons away;
they fly, forgotten, as a dream
dies at the opening day.

O God, our help in ages past,
our hope for years to come,
be Thou our guide while life shall last,
and our eternal home.

It has been wisely said that no thinking person ever regarded the beginning of a new year with indifference. Each of us face many concerns and questions as we stand on the threshold of the unknown future.

The mystery of time is the subject of this hymn text, a paraphrase of Psalm 90. The hymn is considered by many to be one of the finest ever written and perhaps the best known of the six hundred hymns by Isaac Watts, often called the "father of English hymnody."

At an early age Isaac displayed unusual talent in writing poetic verse. As a young man he became increasingly concerned with the congregational singing in the English-speaking churches. Only ponderous metrical psalms were used until this time. To use any words other than the actual words of Scripture would have been considered an insult to God.

Challenged by his father to "write something better for us to sing," young Watts began to

36

create new versions of the psalms with inspiring and expressive style. Eventually, at the early age of twenty-five, he published an important hymnal titled *The Psalms of David in the Language of the New Testament*. In addition to "O God, Our Help in Ages Past," several of Watts' other paraphrases based on psalm settings are hymn texts still widely sung today. They include such favorites as "Joy to the World" (Psalm 98) and "Jesus Shall Reign" (Psalm 72).

After more than two hundred and fifty years, Isaac Watts' hymn is still a timely reminder of God's faithfulness throughout the past and His sure promises for our future.

Isaac Watts.

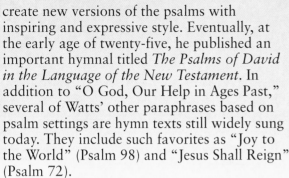

For Today

Psalm 33:20, 48:14, 90; Isaiah 26:4

Live confidently in the assurance that the One who has directed your steps to this moment of time is worthy of your complete trust for the days ahead.

ALL CREATURES OF OUR GOD AND KING

Francis of Assisi, 1182–1226
English Translation by William Draper, 1855–1933

All Thy works shall praise Thee, O Lord; and Thy saints shall bless Thee. They shall speak of the glory of Thy kingdom, and talk of Thy power. (Psalm 145:10–11)

Lasst Uns Erfreuen tune   From the *Geistliche Kirchengesang* of 1623

All creatures of our God and King,
lift up your voice and with us sing
Alleluia, Alleluia!
Thou burning sun with golden beam,
thou silver moon with softer gleam:

Thou rushing wind that art so strong,
ye clouds that sail in heav'n along,
Thou rising morn, in praise rejoice;
ye lights of evening, find a voice:

Dear mother earth, who day by day
unfoldest blessings on our way,
The flow'rs and fruits that in thee grow,
let them His glory also show;

Let all things their Creator bless,
and worship Him in humbleness
Praise, praise the Father, praise the Son,
and praise the Spirit, Three in One:

REFRAIN:
O praise Him, O praise Him!
Alleluia, Alleluia! Alleluia!

All the magnificent wonders of nature reveal the majesty of God and glorify Him. From the grateful heart of a devoted Italian monk in the year of 1225 came this beautiful message. As a great lover of nature, Saint Francis of Assisi saw the hand of God in all creation, and he urged men to respond with expressions of praise and alleluia.

Giovanni Bernardone, the real name of Saint Francis, demonstrated through his own life all the tender, humble, forgiving spirit and absolute trust in God that his hymn urges others to have. At the age of twenty-five Bernardone left an indulgent life as a soldier, renounced his inherited wealth, and determined to live meagerly and to imitate the selfless life of Christ.

Throughout his life Saint Francis appreciated the importance of church music and

38

encouraged singing in his monastery. He wrote more than sixty hymns for this purpose. The beautiful expressions of praise in "All Creatures of Our God and King" have endured throughout the centuries. A prayer written by Saint Francis has also become familiar and well-loved:

Lord, make me an instrument of Thy peace.
Where there is hatred, let me sow love.
Where there is injury, pardon,
Where there is discord, unity.
Where there is doubt, faith.
Where there is error, truth.
Where there is despair, hope.
Where there is sadness, joy.
Where there is darkness, light.
For it is in giving, that we receive.
It is in pardoning, that we are pardoned.
It is in dying, that we are born to eternal life.

For Today

Psalm 145; Jeremiah 32:17–20; Romans 11:36; Revelation 14:7

Praise God continually for His many blessings and for the wonders of His creation.

Francis of Assisi.

39

O LOVE THAT WILL NOT LET ME GO

George Matheson, 1842–1902

I have loved you with an everlasting love; I have drawn you with lovingkindness. (Jeremiah 31:3)

St. Margaret tune

Albert L. Peace, 1844–1912

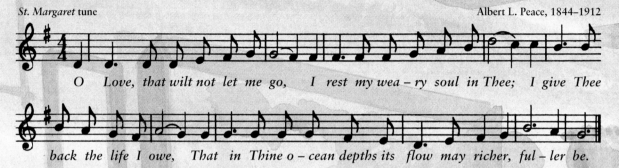

O Love, that wilt not let me go, I rest my wea-ry soul in Thee; I give Thee

back the life I owe, That in Thine o-cean depths its flow may richer, ful-ler be.

O Love, that wilt not let me go,
I rest my weary soul in Thee;
I give Thee back the life I owe,
that in Thine ocean depths
its flow may richer, fuller be.

O Light that follow'st all my way,
I yield my flick'ring torch to Thee;
my heart restores its borrowed ray,
that in Thy sunshine's blaze
its day may brighter, fairer be.

O Joy that seekest me thru pain,
I cannot close my heart to Thee;
I trace the rainbow thru the rain,
and feel the promise is not vain
that morn shall tearless be.

O Cross that liftest up my head,
I dare not ask to fly from Thee;
I lay in dust life's glory dead,
and from the ground there blossoms red
life that shall endless be.

The writing of this thoughtful and artistically constructed text is most remarkable! It was authored by an esteemed Scottish minister who was totally blind and who described the writing as the "fruit of much mental suffering." Many conjectures have been made regarding the cause of the "mental suffering." Fortunately, Dr. George Matheson did leave this account:

My hymn was composed in the manse of Innelan on the evening of the 6th of June, 1882, when I was 40 years of age. I was alone in the manse at that time. It was the night of my sister's marriage, and the rest of the family were staying overnight in Glasgow. Something happened to me, which was known only to myself, and which caused me the most severe mental suffering. The hymn was the fruit of that suffering. It was the quickest bit of work I ever did in my life. I had the impression of having it dictated to me by some inward voice rather than of working it out myself. I am quite sure that the whole work was completed in five minutes, and equally sure that it never received at my hands any retouching or correction. I have no natural gift of rhythm. All the other verses I have ever written are manufactured articles; this came like a dayspring from on high.

A popular account for the writing of this hymn, though never fully substantiated, claims that it was the result of the reminder at his sister's wedding of the great disappointment that Matheson had experienced just before he was to have been married to his college fiancée. When told of his impending total blindness, she is said to have informed him, "I do not wish to be the wife of a blind preacher."

It is very possible that the lingering memory of this rejection from an earthly lover prompted George Matheson to write this beautiful expression of an eternal love that will never be broken.

George Matheson.

For Today

Romans 8:35–39; 1 John 3:1; Revelation 1:5–6

Rest securely in God's eternal love, regardless of the human difficulty or suffering you may be experiencing.

41

GUIDE ME, O THOU GREAT JEHOVAH

William Williams, 1717–1791

Since You are my rock and my fortress, for the sake of Your name lead and guide me. (Psalm 31:3)

Cwm Rhondda tune   John Hughes, 1873–1932

Songs of prais – es, songs of prai – ses, I will ev – er give to

Thee, I will ev – er give to Thee.

Guide me, O Thou great Jehovah,
pilgrim thru this barren land;
I am weak, but Thou art mighty—
Hold me with Thy pow'rful hand:
Bread of Heaven, Bread of Heaven,
feed me till I want no more.

Open now the crystal fountain,
whence the healing stream doth flow;
Let the fire and cloudy pillar
lead me all my journey through;
Strong Deliverer, strong Deliverer,
be Thou still my strength and shield.

When I tread the verge of Jordan,
bid my anxious fears subside;
Bear me thru the swelling current;
land me safe on Canaan's side:
Songs of praises, songs of praises,
I will ever give to Thee.

The need for daily guidance is one of the believer's greatest concerns. How easily our lives can go astray without the assurance of divine leadership. This text is one of the great hymns of the church on this subject. It is a product of the revival movement that swept through Wales during the eighteenth century. This revival was led by a twenty-four-year-old Welsh preacher, Howell Harris, who stirred the land with his fervent evangelistic preaching and his use of congregational singing.

One of the lives touched by Harris's ministry was twenty-year-old William Williams. Young Williams, the son of a wealthy Welsh farmer, was preparing to become a medical doctor. But, upon hearing the stirring challenge by evangelist Howell Harris, Williams dedicated his life to God and the Christian ministry. William Williams, like Harris, decided to take all of Wales as his parish and for the next forty-three years travelled one hundred thousand miles on horseback, preaching and singing the gospel in his native tongue. He became known as the "sweet singer of Wales."

The vivid, symbolic imagery of this text is drawn wholly from the Bible. The setting is the march of the Israelites from Egypt to Canaan. Although the Israelites' sin and unbelief kept them from their destination for forty years, God provided for their physical needs with a new supply of manna each day.

William Williams.

Twice during the Hebrews' years of wandering, they became faint because of lack of water. At the command of God, Moses struck a large rock with his wooden staff. Out of it flowed a pure, crystalline stream that preserved their lives. God also continued to guide them with a pillar of cloud by day and a pillar of fire by night.

For Today

Psalm 16:11, 32:8; Isaiah 58:11; Romans 8:14

Claim God's promises for your life in even the small decisions you will be called upon to make this day.

JESUS, LOVER OF MY SOUL

Charles Wesley, 1707–1788

The Lord is good, a refuge in times of trouble. He cares for those who trust in Him. (Nahum 1:7)

Martyn tune   Simeon B. Marsh, 1798–1875

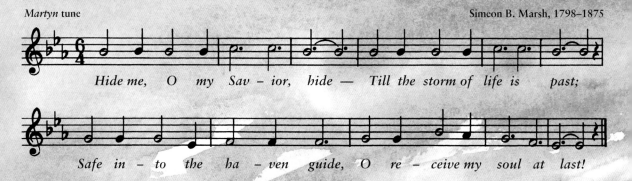

Hide me, O my Sav – ior, hide — Till the storm of life is past;

Safe in – to the ha – ven guide, O re – ceive my soul at last!

Jesus, lover of my soul,
let me to Thy bosom fly.
While the nearer waters roll,
while the tempest still is high!
Hide me, O my Savior, hide—
till the storm of life is past;
safe into the haven guide,
O receive my soul at last!

Other refuge have I none—
hangs my helpless soul on Thee.
Leave, ah, leave me not alone;
still support and comfort me!
All my trust on Thee is stayed—
All my help from Thee I bring.
Cover my defenseless head
with the shadow of Thy wing.

Plenteous grace with Thee is found,
grace to cover all my sin;
let the healing streams abound;
make and keep me pure within.
Thou of life the fountain art—
Freely let me take of Thee;
spring Thou up within my heart;
rise to all eternity.

The universal recognition of a personal dependence upon the infinite God has no doubt made this appealing hymn the best loved of the more than 6,500 texts of Charles Wesley. This text has brought comfort and inspiration to countless numbers during "the storms of life."

The simple yet vivid language of this hymn gives it a special quality. Some have called it the "finest heart-hymn in the English language." Also, the exaltation of Christ is truly noteworthy in such picturesque terms as "lover," "healer," "fountain," "wing," and "pilot." But possibly the greatest appeal of these lines is the assurance they give of Christ's consolation and protection through all of life and then for eternity.

There is no authenticated information as to what particular situation caused Wesley to write this text. A frightening storm at sea that he experienced while returning home from

44

America may account for the nautical references. A story also has been mentioned of a bird flying into Charles's cabin for safety, while another incident is given of his hiding under a hedge after an attack by an angry mob opposing his ministry. Still others see this text as a picture of Wesley's own life as a young man as he struggled to find his peace with God before his dramatic Aldersgate conversion experience.

How important it is that we learn the truth taught in these words!

For Today

Psalm 37:39–40; 2 Corinthians 1:3–7; Revelation 7:17

Remember to fly to Christ for refuge whenever the "storm of life" becomes overwhelming. He alone is our refuge and the one true foundation of life.

O COME, ALL YE FAITHFUL

Latin hymn, 18th century
English Translation by Frederick Oakeley, 1802–1880

When the angels had left them and gone into heaven, the shepherds said to one another, "Let's go to Bethlehem and see this thing that has happened, which the Lord has told us about!"... (Luke 2:15, 20)

Adeste Fideles tune

From Wade's *Cantus Diversi*, 1751

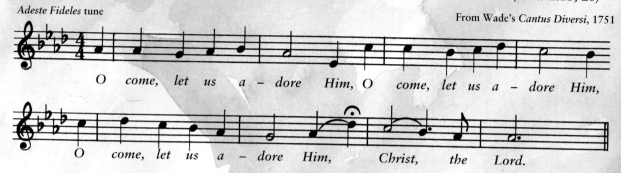

O come, let us a-dore Him, O come, let us a-dore Him,
O come, let us a-dore Him, Christ, the Lord.

O come, all ye faithful,
joyful and triumphant;
come ye, O come ye to Bethlehem;
come and behold Him,
born the King of angels:

Sing, choirs of angels,
sing in exultation;
sing all ye bright hosts of heav'n above;
glory to God,
all glory in the highest:

Yea, Lord, we greet Thee,
born this happy morning;
Jesus, to Thee be all glory giv'n;
Word of the Father,
now in flesh appearing:

REFRAIN:
O come, let us adore Him,
Christ, the Lord.

The songs of the Christmas season comprise some of the finest music known to man, and this hymn is certainly a universal favorite. It was used in Catholic churches before it became known to Protestants. Today it is sung by church groups around the world, having been translated from its original Latin into more than one hundred other languages. The vivid imagery of the carol seems to have meaning and appeal for all ages in every culture.

The original Latin text consists of four stanzas. The first calls us to visualize anew the infant Jesus in Bethlehem's stable. The second stanza, usually omitted from most hymnals, reminds us that the Christ-child is very God Himself:

God of God and Light of Light begotten, Lo, He abhors not the Virgin's womb; Very God, begotten, not created—O come, let us adore Him.

46

The next stanza pictures for us the exalted song of the angelic choir heard by the lowly shepherds. Then the final verse offers praise and adoration to the Word, our Lord, who was with the Father from the beginning of time.

For many years this hymn was known as an anonymous Latin hymn. Recent research, however, has revealed manuscripts that indicate that it was written in 1744 by an English layman named John Wade and set to music by him in much the same style as used today. The hymn first appeared in his collection, *Cantus Diversi*, published in England in 1751. One hundred years later the carol was translated into its present English form by an Anglican minister, Frederick Oakeley, who desired

to use it for his congregation. The tune name, *"Adeste Fideles,"* is taken from the first words of the original Latin text, and translated literally means "be present or near, ye faithful."

For Today

Matthew 2:1–2; Luke 2:9–14; John 1:14

Ask God to help you and your family make the Christmas season a special time for remembering and worshiping "the King of angels."

47

O SACRED HEAD, NOW WOUNDED

Attributed to Bernard of Clairvaux, 1091–1153
Translated into German by Paul Gerhardt, 1607–1676
Translated into English by James W. Alexander, 1804–1859

And when they had plaited a crown of thorns, they put it upon His head, and a reed in His right hand; and they bowed the knee before Him, and mocked Him, saying, "Hail, King of the Jews!" And they spit upon Him, and took the reed, and smote Him on the head. (Matthew 27:29–30 KJV)

Passion Chorale tune

Hans Leo Hassler, 1564–1612

O make me Thine for – ev – er! And, should I faint – ing be,

Lord, let me nev – er, nev – er Out – live my love to Thee!

O sacred Head, now wounded,
with grief and shame weighed down,
now scornfully surrounded
with thorns Thy only crown;
how art Thou pale with anguish,
with sore abuse and scorn!
How does that visage languish
which once was bright as morn!

What language shall I borrow
to thank Thee, dearest Friend,
for this Thy dying sorrow,
Thy pity without end?
O make me Thine forever!
And, should I fainting be,
Lord, let me never, never
outlive my love to Thee!

It is difficult to join our fellow believers each Lenten season in the singing of this passion hymn without being moved almost to tears. For more than eight hundred years these worshipful lines from the heart of a devoted medieval monk have portrayed for parishioners a memorable view of the suffering Savior.

This remarkable text has been generally attributed to Bernard of Clairvaux, the very admirable abbot of a monastery in France. Forsaking the wealth and ease of a noble family for a life of simplicity, holiness, prayer, and ministering to the physical and spiritual needs of others, Bernard was one of the most influential church leaders of his day. Martin Luther wrote of him, "He was the best monk that ever lived, whom I admire beyond all the rest put together."

"O Sacred Head, Now Wounded" was part of the final portion of a lengthy poem that addressed the various parts of Christ's body as He suffered on the cross. The seven sections of the poem considered His feet, knees, hands, side, breast, heart, and face. The stanzas of the hymn were translated into German in the seventeenth century and from German into English in the nineteenth century. God has preserved this exceptional hymn, which has led Christians through the centuries to more ardent worship of His Son.

Bernard of Clairvaux.

For Today

Isaiah 53; Matthew 27:39–43; Philippians 2:8; 1 Peter 3:18

Ponder anew your suffering Savior; then commit your life more fully to Him.

49

PRAISE TO THE LORD, THE ALMIGHTY

Joachim Neander, 1650–1680
Translated by Catherine Winkworth, 1829–1878
Let the people praise Thee, O God; let all the people praise Thee. (Psalm 67:3)

Lobe Den Herren tune

From *Stralsund Gesangbuch*, 1665

All ye who hear, Now to His tem – ple draw near;

Join me in glad ad – o – ra – tion.

Praise to the Lord,
the Almighty, the King of creation!
O my soul, praise Him,
for He is thy health and salvation!
All ye who hear, now to His temple draw near;
join me in glad adoration.

Praise to the Lord,
who o'er all things so wondrously reigneth,
shelters thee under His wings,
yea, so gently sustaineth!
Hast thou not seen how thy desires e'er have been
granted in what He ordaineth?

Praise to the Lord,
who with marvelous wisdom hath made thee,
decked thee with health, and with loving hand
guided and stayed thee;
How oft in grief hath not He brought thee relief,
spreading His wings for to shade thee!

Praise to the Lord!
O let all that is in me adore Him!
All that hath life and breath,
come now with praises before Him!
Let the Amen sound from His people again:
Gladly for aye we adore Him!

Great expressions of praise to God have come from many different traditions and backgrounds. Throughout the centuries God has used the talents of people from various cultures to provide His church with hymns of praise so His people might be known as people of praise and thanksgiving.

The author of this inspiring hymn text, Joachim Neander, has often been called the greatest of all German-Calvinist Reformed hymn writers. He wrote approximately sixty hymns and composed many tunes. Nearly all of his hymns are triumphant expressions of praise.

This hymn is a free paraphrase of Psalm 103:1–6, which begins, "Bless [praise] the Lord, O my soul: And all that is within me, bless His holy name." The translator of this text, Catherine Winkworth, is regarded as one of the finest translators of the German language. Her translations helped to make German hymns popular in England and America during the nineteenth century.

The tune "*Lobe Den Herren*" ("Praise to the Lord") first appeared in a German hymnal in 1665. It is said that Neander personally chose this tune for his text, and the words have never been used with any other melody.

Catherine Winkworth.

For Today

Psalm 100, 103:1–6, 104, 150; Colossians 1:15–20

It has been said that "He who sincerely praises God will soon discover within his soul an inclination to praise goodness in his fellow men." Make this your daily goal.

51

ROCK OF AGES

Augustus M. Toplady, 1740–1778

For I do not want you to be ignorant of the fact, brothers, that our forefathers were all under the cloud and that they all passed through the sea . . . they all ate the same spiritual food and drank the same spiritual drink; for they drank from the spiritual rock that accompanied them and that rock was Christ. (1 Corinthians 10:1, 3–4)

Toplady tune

Thomas Hastings, 1784–1872

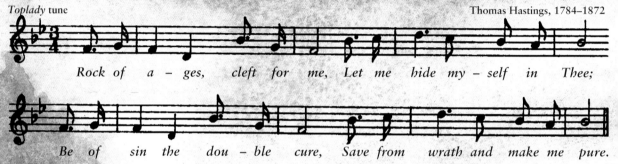

Rock of a-ges, cleft for me, Let me hide my-self in Thee;

Be of sin the dou-ble cure, Save from wrath and make me pure.

Rock of ages, cleft for me,
let me hide myself in Thee;
let the water and the blood,
from Thy wounded side which flowed,
be of sin the double cure,
save from wrath and make me pure.

Could my tears forever flow,
could my zeal no languor know,
these for sin could not atone—
Thou must save and Thou alone:
In my hand no price I bring;
simply to Thy cross I cling.

While I draw this fleeting breath,
when my eyes shall close in death,
when I rise to worlds unknown
and behold Thee on Thy throne,
Rock of Ages, cleft for me,
let me hide myself in Thee.

This fervent plea for Christ our eternal rock to grant salvation through His sacrifice and to be a place of refuge for the believer is one of the most popular hymns ever written. With strong emotional impact, it proclaims Christ's atonement on the cross to be the only means of salvation, making man's tears and efforts to justify himself of no avail. Also it urges us to find consolation and security in Christ our Rock—even at the time of death.

Augustus Toplady's strong and passionate lines were actually written to refute some of the teachings of John and Charles Wesley during a bitter controversy with them concerning Arminianism (which stresses people's free will) versus John Calvin's doctrine of election. "Rock of Ages" was the climax to an article that Toplady wrote in *The Gospel Magazine* in 1776, in which he supported the doctrine of election by arguing that just as England could

52

never pay her national debt, so man through his own efforts could never satisfy the eternal justice of a holy God. Despite the belligerent intent of this text, God has preserved this hymn for more than two hundred years to bring blessing to both Arminian and Calvinistic believers around the world.

At the age of sixteen, as he sat in a barn and listened to the preaching of an uneducated man, Toplady was dramatically converted. Later, he became a powerful and respected minister of the Anglican church. While he was the busy pastor of several churches in England, Augustus Toplady wrote many hymn texts, but few have survived. "Rock of Ages" is the one for which he is best known today.

Augustus M. Toplady.

For Today

Exodus 17:1–6, 33:17–23; Psalm 78:35; Acts 4:12

Give sincere praise to Christ, our "Rock of Ages," for His great gift of salvation and for His provision of a place of refuge for us, even unto death.

SILENT NIGHT! HOLY NIGHT!

Joseph Mohr, 1792–1848
English Translation by John F. Young, 1820–1885
Today in the town of David a Savior has been born to you: He is Christ the Lord. (Luke 2:11)

Stille Nacht tune   Franz Gruber, 1787–1863

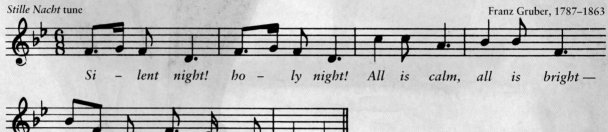

Si - lent night! ho - ly night! All is calm, all is bright —

Sleep in heav - en - ly peace.

Silent night! holy night!
all is calm, all is bright
round yon virgin mother and Child,
holy Infant, so tender and mild—
sleep in heavenly peace.

Silent night! holy night!
shepherds quake at the sight;
glories stream from heaven afar;
heav'nly hosts sing alleluia—
Christ the Savior is born!

Silent night! holy night!
Son of God, love's pure light
radiant beams from Thy holy face
with the dawn of redeeming grace—
Jesus, Lord at Thy birth.

When this beloved hymn was written by two humble church leaders for their own mountain village parishioners, little did they realize how universal its influence would eventually be.

Joseph Mohr, assistant priest in the Church of St. Nicholas in the region of Tyrol, high in the beautiful Alps, and Franz Grüber, the village schoolmaster and church organist, had often talked about the fact that the perfect Christmas hymn had never been written. So Father Mohr had this goal in mind when he received word that the church organ would not function. He decided that he must write his own Christmas hymn immediately in order to have music for the special Christmas Eve mass. He did not want to disappoint his faithful flock. Upon completing the text, he took his words to Franz Grüber, who exclaimed when he saw them, "Friend Mohr, you have found it—the right song—God be praised!"

Soon Grüber completed his task of

composing an appropriate tune for the new text. His simple but beautiful music blended perfectly with the spirit of Father Mohr's words. The carol was completed in time for the Christmas Eve mass, and Father Mohr and Franz Grüber sang their new hymn to the accompaniment of Grüber's guitar. The hymn made a deep impact upon the parishioners even as it has on succeeding generations.

When the organ repairman came to the little village church, he was impressed by a copy of the Christmas carol and decided to spread it all around the region of Tyrol. Today it is sung in all major languages of the world and is a favorite wherever songs of the Christmas message are enjoyed.

Joseph Mohr.

For Today

Matthew 2:9–10; Luke 1:77–79; Luke 2:7–20

Allow the peaceful strains of this carol to help you worship in awe with the shepherds and sing alleluia with the angels for God's "redeeming grace."

55

WHAT A FRIEND WE HAVE IN JESUS

Joseph Scriven, 1819–1886

A man that hath friends must show himself friendly: And there is a friend that sticketh closer than a brother. (Proverbs 18:24 KJV)

Converse tune

Charles C. Converse, 1832–1918

O what peace we oft-en for-feit, O what need-less pain we bear,

All be-cause we do not car-ry Ev-'ry thing to God in prayer.

What a Friend we have in Jesus,
all our sins and griefs to bear!
What a privilege to carry
everything to God in prayer!
O what peace we often forfeit,
O what needless pain we bear,
all because we do not carry
everything to God in prayer.

Are we weak and heavy laden,
cumbered with a load of care?
Precious Savior, still our refuge—
Take it to the Lord in prayer.
Do thy friends despise, forsake thee?
Take it to the Lord in prayer;
in His arms He'll take and shield thee—
Thou wilt find a solace there.

A true friend loves and accepts us just as we are, stays close to us in good or in bad, and is always ready to help in time of need. Because the author of this hymn text found just such a friend in his Lord, he decided to spend his entire life showing real friendship to others.

Joseph Scriven had wealth, education, a devoted family, and a pleasant life in his native Ireland. Then unexpected tragedy entered. On the night before Scriven's scheduled wedding, his fiancée drowned. In his deep sorrow, Joseph realized that he could find the solace and support he needed only in his dearest friend, Jesus.

Soon after this tragedy, Scriven dramatically changed his lifestyle. He left Ireland for Port Hope, Canada, determined to devote all of his extra time in being a friend and helper to others. He often gave away his clothing and possessions to those in need, and he worked—

without pay—for anyone who needed him. Scriven became known as "the Good Samaritan of Port Hope."

When Scriven's mother became ill in Ireland, he wrote a comforting letter to her, enclosing the words of his newly written poem with the prayer that these brief lines would remind her of a never-failing heavenly Friend. Sometime later, when Joseph Scriven himself was ill, a friend who came to call on him happened to see a copy of these words scribbled on scratch paper near his bed. The friend read the lines with interest and asked, "Who wrote those beautiful words?"

"The Lord and I did it between us," was Scriven's reply.

For Today

Psalm 6:9; Mark 11:24; John 15:13–16; 1 John 5:14–15

Like Joseph Scriven, we too can find relief from our burdens when we turn to our Lord as a friend.

57

O FOR A THOUSAND TONGUES

Charles Wesley, 1707–1788

Let everything that has breath praise the Lord. Praise the Lord. (Psalm 150:6)

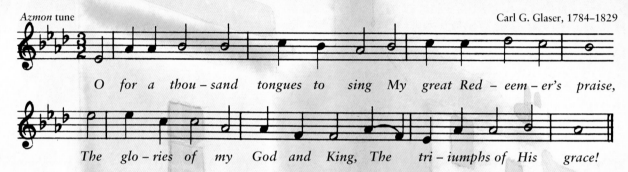

Azmon tune

Carl G. Glaser, 1784–1829

O for a thou-sand tongues to sing My great Red-eem-er's praise,

The glo-ries of my God and King, The tri-umphs of His grace!

O for a thousand tongues to sing
my great Redeemer's praise,
the glories of my God and King,
the triumphs of His grace.

My gracious Master and my God,
assist me to proclaim,
to spread thru all the earth abroad
the honors of Thy name.

Jesus! the name that charms our fears,
that bids our sorrows cease,
'tis music in the sinner's ears;
'tis life and health and peace.

He breaks the pow'r of canceled sin;
He sets the pris'ner free.
His blood can make the foulest clean . . .
His blood availed for me.

Hear Him, ye deaf, His praise, ye dumb,
your loosened tongues employ;
ye blind, behold your Savior come
and leap ye lame, for joy.

Soon after their graduation from Oxford University, John and Charles Wesley decided to sail to America, the New World, to try to minister to the rough colonists under General Oglethorpe in Georgia and to evangelize the Indians. The Wesleys soon became disillusioned with the situation there, however, and after a short time returned to England.

As they crossed the Atlantic, John and Charles were much impressed by a group of devout Moravians, who seemed to have such spiritual depth and vitality as well as genuine missionary zeal. After returning to London, the Wesleys met with a group of Moravians in the Aldersgate Hall. Here in May 1738, both brothers had a spiritual "heart-warming experience," realizing that even though they had been so zealous in religious activity, neither had ever personally known God's forgiveness or real joy. From that time on their ministry displayed a new dimension of spiritual power.

"O for a Thousand Tongues" was written by Charles in 1749 on the eleventh anniversary of his Aldersgate conversion experience. It was inspired by a chance remark of an influential Moravian leader named Peter Bohler, who expressed his spiritual joy in this way: "Oh, Brother Wesley, the Lord has done so much for my life. Had I a thousand tongues, I would praise Christ Jesus with every one of them!"

These words of personal testimony by Charles Wesley have provided a moving vehicle of worship for God's people for more than two centuries.

For Today

Psalm 96:1–4, 103:1–4, 145:2–3; Romans 14:17

Let this hymn be the desire of your heart as you meditate on its words.

WHEN I SURVEY THE WONDROUS CROSS

Isaac Watts, 1674–1748

Carrying His own cross, He went out to the place of the Skull (which in Aramaic is called Golgotha).
Here they crucified Him. (John 19:17–18)

Hamburg tune

Arr. by Lowell Mason, 1792–1872

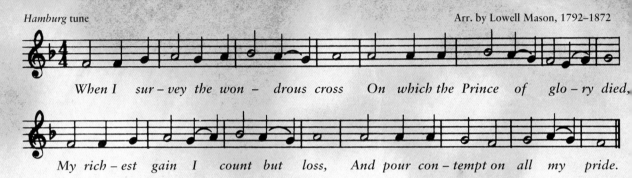

When I sur – vey the won – drous cross   On which the Prince of glo – ry died,

My rich – est gain I count but loss,   And pour con – tempt on all my pride.

When I survey the wondrous cross
on which the Prince of glory died,
my richest gain I count but loss,
and pour contempt on all my pride.

Forbid it, Lord, that I should boast,
save in the death of Christ, my God;
all the vain things that charm me most—
I sacrifice them to His blood.

See, from His head, His hands, His feet,
sorrow and love flow mingled down;
did e'er such love and sorrow meet,
or thorns compose so rich a crown?

Were the whole realm of nature mine,
that were a present far too small:
Love so amazing, so divine,
demands my soul, my life, my all.

While preparing for a communion service in 1707, Isaac Watts wrote this deeply moving and very personal expression of gratitude for the amazing love that the death of Christ on the cross revealed. It first appeared in print that same year in Watts' outstanding collection, *Hymns and Spiritual Songs*. The hymn was originally titled "Crucifixion to the World by the Cross of Christ." Noted theologian Matthew Arnold called this the greatest hymn in the English language. In Watts' day, texts such as this, which were based only on personal feelings, were termed "hymns of human composure" and were very controversial, since almost all congregational singing at this time consisted of ponderous repetitions of the Psalms. The unique thoughts presented by Watts in these lines certainly must have pointed the eighteenth-century Christians to a view of the dying Savior in a vivid and memorable way that led them to a deeper worship experience, even as it does for us today.

Young Watts showed unusual talent at an early age, learning Latin when he was five, Greek at nine, French at eleven and Hebrew at twelve. As he grew up, he became increasingly disturbed by the uninspiring psalm singing in the English churches. He commented, "The singing of God's praise is the part of worship most closely related to heaven; but its performance among us is the worst on earth." Throughout his life, Isaac Watts wrote over six hundred hymns and is known today as the "father of English hymnody." His hymns were strong and triumphant statements of the Christian faith, yet none ever equalled the colorful imagery and genuine devotion of this emotionally stirring and magnificent hymn text.

For Today

Matthew 26:28; Luke 7:47; Romans 5:6–11; Galatians 6:14

Can you say with Isaac Watts: "my soul, my life, my all"?

Index of first lines

Index of authors

AMAZING GRACE:
366 Inspiring Hymn Stories for Daily Devotions
0-8254-3425-4

A national best-selling devotional book with more than 200,000 copies in print! Each of the 366 selections presents an inspiring, true-life experience behind the writing of a well-known hymn and the biblical truths drawn from it. Each day's selection includes a portion of the hymn, as well as suggested Scripture readings and meditations.

101 HYMN STORIES
0-8254-3416-5

Perfect for devotions, sermon illustrations, bulletin inserts, and congregational hymn introductions, each hymn story includes information about the author or composer, and the scriptural background of the hymn. Some of the favorites included are: "A Mighty Fortress," "Fairest Lord Jesus," "How Great Thou Art," "Rock of Ages," and "This Is My Father's World."

101 MORE HYMN STORIES
0-8254-3420-3

This companion volume to *101 Hymn Stories* contains 101 more stories behind favorite hymns that will warm your heart and revitalize your worship. Some of the hymns included are: "Turn Your Eyes Upon Jesus," "Trust and Obey," "I Surrender All," "Burdens Are Lifted at Calvary," and "Because He Lives."

25 MOST TREASURED GOSPEL HYMN STORIES
0-8254-3430-0

Along with each story about the writing of twenty-five popular gospel hymns is a Scripture passage, a thoughtful reflection, and the full musical score, all of which lend greater meaning to these all-time favorites. Some of the gospel hymns included are: "His Eye Is on the Sparrow," "It Is Well with My Soul," "Precious Lord, Take My Hand," and "Since Jesus Came Into My Heart."

Available at your local bookstore or by calling 800-733-2607